Between 2003 and 2021 I had the honour of preaching at a number of Baptist churches as a lay preacher. Due to health reasons in recent years I have stood down as a Baptist preacher and have joined the local Anglican church, where I serve on the PCC leadership.

I have put together a few of my old sermons in this short book to encourage and help build each other up.

All sermon's in this book were written and spoke during the time I was a Baptist preacher.

As you read these sermons I pray you get a sense of the Holy Spirit speaking to you as you either preach or are looking into preaching.

Be encouraged on your journey.

Tim

Sermon One

Matthew 7 v 7 to 12 and Matthew 7 v 24-29

Before my Dad entered into Baptist ministry he was head of electronics at Southmead hospital in Bristol, one day he shared with me how a new member of staff had just graduated from university and was quite arrogant and would wind the other members of staff up. My Dad being my Dad took this particular member of staff to one side and asked her if she would go to the petrol station as and get some petrol powder. The lady without question went along to the garage and asked for some petrol powder, Dad never told me too much what happened after that but one can only imagine.

This morning we have looked at the passage which looks at asking, seeking and knocking at the door. A lot of people have taken this passage out of context in times past particularly verse 8, 'for everyone who asks receives'. People have taken this literally to mean whatever they get and this is not what Jesus is actually saying. Just like the lady with the petrol powder, we must look properly at what is being said here and apply it. Matthew 7 is commonly called 'the sermon on the mount', it is a description of a truly righteous life and an outlining law of Christ. When Jesus said, 'ask and it will be given to you', he had continued prayer in his mind, prayer is the essential way in which we communicate with God. Of course God is forever present but he has given us the gift of prayer as a way of communication and a way of bringing about answers. Sometimes those answers are not quite what we are anticipating or wanting at the time but I can testify personally to how God knows best and has a plan for us.

Jesus is *not* saying that believers always get what they ask for—wrong motives, for example, will hinder answers to prayer (James 4:3). However, the more time a Christian spends in communion with God, the more he or she will know what to ask for in accordance with God's will.

When Jesus said 'seek and find' he was talking about God himself.

I believe there a number of things we can take from the passages we have read this morning.

1. As church (in general) we must get back to the basics and seek the Kingdom of God through prayer

Jesus then said, "Knock and the door will be opened to you" (Matthew 7:7c). Here, the Lord uses a metaphor for the action a desire produces. If a person needs something from someone behind a door, the most natural thing to do is knock—and keep knocking until the door is opened and the desire is met. In the same way, a believer should pray in faith for God's provision and be persistent in prayer (see Luke 18:1).

It is my firm conviction during these past 18 months that we as a church have a great opportunity of reaching out to our communities and sharing the love of God with so many hurting people but before we can do any of this we have to seek first the Kingdom of God and then all these things will be added unto us. The lost will be found and many lives will be transformed. The most important thing we can do is to pray whether that be on our own, in groups or prayer days. I had the joy of coming along to your prayer day the other month and that was a huge encouragement to myself because it reminded me of the most important reason why we are here, to glorify God. I get excited when I see a church in action with it's prayer life as this is the heart beat of the church and who we are.

God delights in the prayer of faith, and He promises to give us what we need. There is a huge difference between wants and needs. As a parent I find myself in this battle quite regularly particularly when we are out and about doing shopping. Quite often our children are saying things like 'I want this and that' and as parents we are having to correct them for their own good. Not that long ago while in a local supermarket Joshua got hold of a packet of paracetomol and put them into the shopping trolley. I of course put them back as they would do a toddler a lot of harm! Sometimes if we are honest enough we have gone to God and asked for things which we want rather than perhaps what we need and the answer has not been quite been what we thought. Just like I knew best for Joshua as his Dad, God knows best for us both as individuals and as a church.

2. When we pray we are building a foundation for the future

Jesus in chapter 7 of the passage we have read this morning went on to say that whoever hears the words which he has spoken is like a wise man who built his house upon rock.

Recently we have had our garden transformed and turf laid down. The advise we were given was to water that turf and not to stand on it for two weeks. Just like we demonstrated with the children's talk, we must water and feed ourselves through prayer if we are to grow. That is a true foundation to build upon and we also must remember it is God's timing and not ours. Being the summer holidays we were desperate for the children to go and play on the new turf however if we had rushed that would have undone a lot of hard work. In the same way as a church, we must not rush but seek the Kingdom of God and in his time things will come together.

We are in a fast paced society where everything must be done now. This has caused no ends of problems for many people and I include myself in that. There are times where I have been so busy I have neglected the basics. I look back over a number of things in my own life and wonder how a better outcome may have been if I had not rushed and slowed down. Slowing down, spending time seeking God's face is essential to our spiritual growth both as a church and individuals. Imagine doing a prayer day like you did the other month say once a month and the long term of that. My friends, I can promise you with such a foundation like this great things will happen as a result.

I know that this church has many faithful praying people and that is why you are building a solid foundation here at Herne Bay and this morning I want to encourage each and every one of us to continue with this and that can done here at the church, in our homes, workplaces or wherever we are in our daily lives.

Failing to keep a solid prayer life in a church can only lead to what Jesus said in the passage we have looked at this morning and that is building upon sand rather than rock.

3. **We may be fearful for the future but this foundation will be build us up**

There has and is a lot of fear in the media, you only have to read a newspaper, go online to certain news channels and I can guarantee your find yourself feeling negative quite quickly.

We all have a certain amount of fear in us and having travelled the journey myself of anxiety following my Dad's death two years ago, I can say personally how much fear really can hold a grip on us. Fear of the future, the unknown these are just a couple of examples of what we go through in life.

During the past 18 months I have personally found I have increased my Bible study and prayer time but it is still nowhere near where it should be. When I let fear get hold of me, looking back my prayer and Bible study life were lacking. I still get fears and I think if we are honest we all do to a certain extent but I have found when praying, reading the Bible and worshipping God, that fear has either gone or is a lot less.

As we look to the future here at Herne Bay, you may have many fears, that could be financial, practical, health or any other things which come to mind however like I have said a few moments ago, if we build ourselves as individuals and as a church on prayer and Bible study, we will be building a foundation that will build us up as individuals and as a community.

It really does excite me to know that when a foundation is being built something beautiful is the end result. That beauty is when we see lives changed and come to know Jesus as their Lord and saviour. The rock which we build upon is Jesus Christ and nothing else. No agenda of our own but only the agenda of seeing the Kingdom of God grow.

Ask, Jesus will make known in his time.

Seek, we will find lost souls.

Knock, the doors to people within our community will open.

When we do this, we are going to witness something very amazing and powerful.

Let's get back to the basics, that is Seeking the kingdom of God through prayer and studying his word.

The closing song I have chosen, 'I will build my church', that is happening and going to continue to happen as long as we keep praying and seeking God's will for us both as individuals and as a church.

Amen.

Sermon Two

2 Kings chapter 2 v 1-25

Elijah and Elisha are the most notable prophets from scripture helping to restore Israel in a time of wicked rulers. Elijah and Elisha traversed the Jordan River on dry land, and Elisha, understanding that Elijah would soon pass away, asked to be blessed with a double portion of Elijah's spirit. Elijah was then carried straight into heaven by a chariot of fire. Elisha picked up Elijah's mantle and used it to cross the Jordan again on dry land. He received the double portion he had asked for and performed many miracles in Israel. Some of Elisha's miracles were the turning of bad water into clean water (2 Kings 2:19-22), making a widow's oil to fill many jars (2 Kings 4:1-7), and even raising a boy from the dead (2 Kings 4:32-37).

This morning as we celebrate mother's day we perhaps come with many mixed emotions. For example for me personally I have not seen my mum for nearly a year due to the pandemic and last weekend she was rushed into hospital and I felt useless. This has been the same for a number of people who have had parents unwell and unable to see them, parents who have even passed away and not been able to be with them. Sadly a number of my colleagues in the ambulance service have seen this full on and the effects it has had. Or perhaps some of us are with our mothers today and that brings a great feeling. Whatever our situation, our mothers bring much comfort and love whether that is physically or at a distance. Even at my age I am told my mum does not stop worrying about me.

As I was preparing this morning's message I really could see a number of things we can take from this passage today particularly being mother's day.

1. **Our mothers never stop caring for us and so it is with God, he cares for us no matter what and where we are**

A number of years ago before I started my work as chaplain to the ambulance service, I served chaplain to a dementia care home in Gravesend. One day I was playing my guitar and a resident was sitting with her daughter joining in with the singing and when we had finished the the joy on both their faces was great to witness. As the daughter was leaving the mother, you could see the tears in the daughter and mother's eyes as they were departing, it really was an emotional thing to witness.

In the chapter we have read this morning Elisha did not want to depart from Elijah and that must have been a powerful bond between the two of them. Elijah cared for Elisha that much and God wants each and everyone of us to know this morning that we are deeply cared and loved for by God.

In this fast paced society we can easily miss the basics of life and caring for one another. One of the things for me personally during this pandemic has been to learn to slow down and remember our first love and that is God. In verse 10 of the opening Psalm this morning we read, "**Be still, and know** that I **am God**". When we come to a place of stillness we can sense God moving in and through us, sometimes we may not even realise it but God is moving amongst us. When we allow ourselves to be still we form that bond with God just like Elijah and Elisha, a bond of God's unconditional love among them.

Back in 2019 my Dad went to be with the Lord in glory and that was both a painful and a powerful experience for me personally. I would say I had a special bond with my Dad (and mum of course) and that departing was painful, causing all sorts of emotions yet I know that Dad safe and well in heaven and I have like all of us here this morning still have a job to do here on earth. Elisha carried on when Elijah went to be with the Lord and God really used him in a powerful way. I want to encourage anybody this morning who may have lost a loved one and is feeling that pain, God cares deeply for you and the tears are a sign of the love and bond which you shared and do share.

It is interesting Darren is doing this series on not complaining, I must admit I am one of the worst for this and have found this a real challenge at times. When my Dad passed away I found myself complaining inside in a number of different ways, for example, 'how could you allow this to happen', 'where is my future' and yet God has clearly been with us as a family even amongst the most difficult times and is beginning to open doors which we never imagined or dreamed of. I personally can testify to the verse in Psalm 30v11, **"You turned my wailing into dancing"**. After Dad's departing came a lot of complaining and that complaining my friends I can reassure you has now turned into praise and thanks, yes I still get my challenging days and grief to a certain extent never leaves us but we can be thankful to God for the bond we have with our parents, if anybody may have had a difficult relationship with their parents please remember God does care deeply for you.

2. God has an amazing plan for our future both as a church and individuals

Jeremiah 29 v 31, For I know the plans I have for you," declares the LORD, "plans to prosper you and not to harm you, plans to give you hope and a future.

This particular verse was the verse of the year for us as a family in 2019 and I must admit at the time I found that very hard to understand.

Elisha would have had many different emotions knowing that Elijah would soon be departing this World and probably could only see the here and now. So it is even now with ourselves, we can only see the current situation and past that.

I want to encourage you as a church this morning because what you have done in this pandemic with these services and other things has really stepped up a gear in a very difficult time and making the future secure. I have personally been attracted online to your services because even online I have sensed a love and caring community and that my friends is to be taken as an encouragement going into the future. Yes the future is very unknown but like Elisha, he would have gone into the unknown when Elijah departed but as we read on into how Elisha was used by God, we can see many doors opened and lives transformed as a result. I firmly believe this during this pandemic that if we are open to God and form that bond which we have spoken about this morning, our own lives as well as many other will be transformed.

Verse 14 to 15 of the chapter we have looked at today, 'Elisha took the mantle of Elijah that had fallen with him and stood at the bank of the river Jordan, striking the water and as a result Elisha was able to cross over'.

Before this happened Elisha must have had anxieties and yet God still made a way and revealed the sign to Elisha that he was still with him. We have many anxieties during this time and it is right that we ask God for signs, signs of where he is leading us and my friends I firmly believe God will reveal these signs to us and we will come through these times and be stronger for it both as individuals and as a church.

As a family we are not planning to live where we are at the moment for many years and to a certain extent we feel in a place of uncertainty yet at the same time I personally have an inward peace that God is going to reveal things in his time and in his ways. Yes we will have challenges on the way but like Elisha, God will open up the waters so we can cross that sea.

3. **God is going to use his church for healing in our communities**

V20-22, The people of the city said to Elisha, "Look, our lord, this town is well situated, as you can see, but the water is bad and the land is unproductive."

20 "Bring me a new bowl," he said, "and put salt in it." So they brought it to him.

21 Then he went out to the spring and threw the salt into it, saying, "This is what the LORD says: 'I have healed this water. Never again will it cause death or make the land unproductive.'" **22** And the water has remained pure to this day, according to the word Elisha had spoken.

It is my firm belief that as a church we have a wonderful opportunity now more than ever to share Jesus and his transforming love and healing power.

There has been so much pain particular during these past few months and each one of us are affected by this. Covid like the bad water in the passage this morning can has really caused so much pain and yet God is offering us a bowl with salt this morning, a salt of healing that can be sprinkled into our communities, that is found in how we love and care for one another. We need to first and foremost sprinkle that love within our church and that will then spread.

My friends I know what pain can be caused by people putting you down and this morning if anybody has an urge to complain about anything, I would suggest just be still before God and lay that complaint to him. It is so easy for us to engage our mouths before we engage our brains, if we could just but be still before God before engaging our mouths, I am certain a lot of unnecessary hurt would not happen.

I have attended many 999 calls with various ambulance crews as part of my work as chaplain to the service and one particular calls always stands out in my mind. We were called to a patient and when we hooked up the ECG unit to the patient it was obvious that the patient was having a heart attack. The patients son was quite aggressive and adamant that his mum wasn't having a heart attack! He then went on to a slanging match with my colleague and I have to press the man down button on the radio which gets police assistance, this resulted in the man getting into a lot of trouble. This is an example of how by engaging our mouths before our brains can cause all sorts of problems. We must always go back to that what I said earlier and BE STILL BEFORE GOD and wait upon him to see what he is saying.

When we throw the fresh salt of water into our church and into our own lives, we can only be pure before God and that will then attract people, people will want to know what it is we have that they don't have and that is a powerful message.

A mother's love is unconditional and yes there are times a mother has to correct us but no matter what we have done that love never dies. God's love for you and I this morning never dies no matter what we have done and where we come from.

Remember this week to ask God for that bowl and to fill it up with fresh salt so that we can sprinkle that amongst one another.

Sermon three

Luke 7:11-16

On a dark and stormy night, an American, a Canadian and a Scotsman were in a bad car accident. All three were rushed to the hospital, though all three had died before they arrived. Just as they were about to put the toe tag on the American, he awoke and opened his eyes. Astonished, the doctors and nurses asked him what had happened.

The American replied, "I remember the crash, and then there was a bright white light, and then the Canadian and the Scotsman and I were standing at the Pearly Gates. St. Peter approached us and said that we were all too young to die, and that for a donation of $150 we could return to earth. So of course I pulled out my wallet and gave him the $150 and the next thing I knew I was back here".

One of the doctors said, "That's amazing, but what happened to the other two?"

The American replied, "Last I saw them, the Scotsman was haggling over the price, and the Canadian was waiting for the government to pay his."

Picture the scene in today's Gospel reading for a moment. The widow has just lost her only son. Since her husband is already dead, she is facing dire personal and financial trouble. In those days, widows were supported by the eldest son. To make matters worse, her son is being buried within 24 hours of his death, as was the custom at that time because of the problem of decomposition combined with the heat. She has not had time to even begin to comprehend the meaning of her loss.

As the funeral procession is leaving the village, Jesus and his followers arrive from the village of Nain. They immediately stop to let the funeral procession pass, something which many of us do today, although there are some who don't. When Jesus sees what is happening, he is moved by compassion. He comforts the widow, and then brings her son back to life.

I grew up in Norwich and we lived next to the church which had quite a lot of land, most weeks I would play football on the land with friends and one particular friend would each week insist that God never existed and I would alway's try to make him think differently. As time went on I felt that there was no hope in my friend coming to know Jesus, a few years after we left Norwich I received a message to say that my friend was going to be baptisted, I remember thinking this took a miracle and I believe Jesus moved in my friend's heart and performed a miracle.

Miracles can be instant and sometimes they can be over a period of time.

The most profound of all the miracles Jesus performed during His earthly ministry are those in which He *resurrected* someone. The New Testament records three of these resurrection miracles, including the raising of a widow's son, of Jairus' daughter, and of Lazarus. Luke the physician is the only one to record the raising of a widow's son (Luke 7:11-17). It is interesting that each of the three resurrection miracles reports the dead person in a different stage of death from the other instances. When Christ raises Jairus' daughter to life, she is still in the bed where she had died only a few hours earlier. The widow's son lies in an open coffin on his way to his grave when Jesus performs the miracle. Finally, Lazarus is already in the grave and has been dead for four days by the time Christ arrives and raises him from the dead (John 11:39).

The varying length of times they had been dead and yet were still resurrected shows that Christ can raise the dead no matter what. His miraculous power to resurrect is not dependent upon whether a person has just died, has been dead for days, or is already decomposing. The same principle holds true regarding spiritual salvation: God and Christ can save any sinner no matter how old he is, how long he has been a sinner, or how badly he has sinned.

I believe there are a number of lesson's which we can learn from the passage we have read this morning when Jesus raised the widow's son.

1. Jesus proved he is the resurrection and the life

The incident we just read about, took place in the city of Nain. Nain is a small village in the plain of Jezreel, about 25 miles south of Capernaum. The village is still known by the same name, which means "pleasant." It is truly a beautiful area, yet people die even in beautiful places. The incident happened near the gate of the city, however the city had never been fortified, so the term "gate" may simply mean a spot where the houses of the town ended and the road began.

It was usually outside of town and some distance away, where the dead were buried. They had different customs, depending upon their age, for carrying out those that were to be buried. A child under a month old was carried in the arms of a person. If the child was a full month old it was placed in a little coffin, which was carried in their arms. A child of twelve months old was carried in a little coffin on the shoulder. And a child that was three years old was carried on a stretcher or bed. This is the way that this corpse was carried, through the gate and out of the city.

Two groups of people met at the gate of Nain, that day. One group, consisting of Jesus and His disciples, was coming toward the city from Capernaum, probably by way of Nazareth. It wasn't only the twelve who accompanied Jesus, but there were many others including some that lived in Capernaum, who followed Him in anticipation of seeing a miracle, like a few hours earlier when Jesus healed a Centurion's servant.

The other group consisted of the widow, whose boy had died, and a great multitude of mourners. If we could only travel back in time to that day, and join the crowd by the gate, we might have observed the whole thing. Allow me to describe the scene to you.

The funeral procession was large, which was typical of a boy that was popular and may have been a local favorite, known by many. Those that were to bear the coffin, most likely had assistants, who were obliged to accompany them, and they changed bearers, if they had to go a great distance, which was often the case. There were some that went before the casket, and others went after it. What's more, there were traditions that worked to increase the size of funeral processions. Those that could afford it, employed professional mourners, who continually cried out how wonderful the person was, and how great a tragedy his death was. Also, it was considered an act of kindness and mercy to follow a corpse to the grave. What's more, there was a prohibition against doing any work, while someone was being buried, even if he was a common person.

The whole town must have felt sorry for this mother for having lost her only boy. It was a scene of great sorrow and mourning, made worse, because the dead son was an only son. No family accompanied the lone woman, since she was widowed and without a family.

2. Jesus is personally involved in miracles

Jesus knew everything about the situation with the widow yet his disciples only could see a funeral taking place as they passed through. Jesus knew that the deceased was a young man, the only son of his mother, and that she is a widow!

Jesus shows compassion and Christ's concern was apparent in His expression of His mercy and tenderness, **verse 13, When the Lord saw her, his heart went out to her and he said, "Don't cry".**

Within my own life there have been many times when I have felt the compassion of Jesus which nobody else could offer for example the other week when I was having my first infusion I was very anxious and while waiting in the infusion lounge receving treatment I felt a peace which I cannot describe, other than it was the Holy Spirit working within me. A few year's ago as I was suffering from PTSD I could not see a way ahead yet I am standing here this morning and I know this is through the Holy Spirit showing compassion upon me and my family, his grace and love is such a a wonderful thing and when Jesus is involved with our situations he will see him working many miracles within our lives and others.

Jesus want's to come alongside us and be involved with our situations because he has compassion, he said to the widow "do not weep", that must have been a real comfort to the woman, we not know how long she has been a widow but presuming her husband had passed away recently it would have been an awful feeling losing her son as well and intensifyed the feelings within so Jesus come's alongside her and comforts her.

This story of the widows son was a miracle done for our sake, to show what takes place when Jesus touches a person who is dead spiritually because of sin. Jesus touched the life of this lady and many others.

3. The chief purpose of performing a resurrection was and is to glorify God

This miracle produces fear in those who witness it, but this fear turns into a deep feeling of awe for His compassion and power. As a result, Christ's fame among the people grows, while the hatred of the Jewish leaders increases, as they reject His claims to be the Son of God.

However, His primary purpose is to glorify God. The people glorify God when they say, "A great prophet has risen up among us" and "God has visited His people." Christ is the Great Prophet of Israel (Deuteronomy 18:15; Luke 3:16; John 6:14). The tragedy in this situation is that, though a number of people look upon Jesus as the promised Prophet, few give Him much devotion.

In their praise, we see gratitude as they glorified God for favoring them with this great blessing.

I recently received an award at Westminster Central Methodist Hall for my work as Chaplain to the Paramedics in Medway and I must admit I felt very overwhelmed at response given to myself. One of the concern's I had and could have easily slipped into was self praise and lapping up the praise but I needed and do remind myself that all of this which any of us do is for the Glory of God.

As we have come to worship this morning, what are our motives?

When we come to Church each week we must learn from this story of the Widow that all we do is for God's glory and we must glorify God in our praises both on a Sunday and in our daily lives.

Each time I go on duty with the Paramedics I pray quietly within my heart before each job that everything I say and do will be to glorify God as I know within my own strength I would not be capable of doing this.

Within our praises we not only need to glorify God but show gratitude, we see in the story of the widow that the people showed gratitude towards Jesus.

Within our society just saying simple things such as thank you can really be a witness.

4. We have a hope

Some of us know the anguish of losing a loved one. You have lost a child. Or an infant. Or a preborn child. All of us know someone who has died. The question we ask is: Does God provide any comfort for grieving people? And, is there any hope beyond the grave? This is a question I have asked myself time and time again over the past few years especially when I suffered from PTSD as a result of the death of a child in our previous church.

Luke answers these questions when he tells us what Jesus did for the grieving mother who lost her only son, and we learn about Jesus' compassion, his power over death, and the response he inspires.

I have condensed the passage down to 5 examples of the hope which Luke answers within this chapter:

1. The Setting of the Miracle (7:11-12)

2. The Compassion of Jesus (7:13)

3. The Power of Jesus (7:14-15)

4. The Response of the People (7:16-17)

5. The Setting of the Miracle (7:11-12)

Luke has included this encounter in his Gospel because he wants us to understand that Jesus still cares for us today. Regardless of the pain and suffering and sorrow and loss we experience, Jesus cares. The same Jesus who had compassion on the widow of Nain reaches out to us in our pain and suffering and sorrow and loss. Isaiah the prophet said, "Surely he has borne our griefs and carried our sorrows" (Isaiah 53:4).

Notice when he spoke to the boy's cold corpse, the boy heard him. The young man was dead in body, but he was fully alive somewhere! For we humans, death is only death of the body. The human spirit lives on." I think it may have been C. S. Lewis who said that we tend to think of ourselves as bodies having souls when in fact we are really souls who have bodies. The point that C.S Lewis is making is that the real "us" is not our bodies but it is our souls. Our bodies die but our souls never die.

By raising the dead young man to life, Jesus was pointing to the death of death in his own future resurrection. Jesus came to destroy death and give us new life and new hope in him. This miracle shows us that Jesus has power over death.

A few years later Jesus was crucified. He died and was buried. But three days later, he was raised back to life. Now that he himself has risen from the dead, he has the power to grant eternal life to anyone who comes to him in faith and repentance. His resurrection is the promise and proof of our own resurrection.

What a hope we all have this morning as we put our trust in the Lord Jesus Christ, that one day we shall spend eternity with our Lord and Saviour.

As each and everyone of us looks to the future in our own personal lives and as a church, let us rejoice that we all have the same hope in Jesus Christ.

Just as the passage we have read this morning says, that we should glorify God let us glorify God both today and for each and every day of our lives.

Let us wholeheartly worship and glorify God in our closing song this morning.

Amen.

Sermon Four

Growing up in Norwich we had some land behind the church which had a few trees, during one school holiday myself, my middle brother and a friend decided to build a tree house, borrowing hammers and nails to bang pieces of wood into the tree (to this day I am not sure my parents knew anything about this) we were having fun. While we were in the middle of this my brother told me to keep lookout for anybody coming as I discovered we were not meant to build tree houses. I noticed a policeman in the distance walking down the road, warned my brother and friend, to which they did not believe me, in the meantime I casually walked off and never was caught in the act, however my brother and friend were, both my brother and friend did not believe me when I warned them.

While preparing for this mornings message this story from my childhood reminded me of the passage we have looked at this morning, Mary treasured and she pondered what the shepherds had said. The shepherds were spreading the good news about Jesus birth and Mary was pondering things over in her heart and mind.

We have just celebrated Christmas, let me ask a question, how many of us have taken serious time this Christmas and pondered what the true story is all about? We get so bogged down into the commercial side of things and it becomes easy to forget the real reason for the season.

In society we are under immense pressure all of the time, for example I serve as Chaplain to the Ambulance Service, this Monday just gone I did a 13 hour shift and we had a number of calls including a death, the process should be after such a job we have an allocated time to discuss about the call but due to pressures we face, we are sent immediately to another job with no time to reflect upon what had happened. This constant pressure is not only in the Ambulance Service but in society in general.

As we enter into a new year I believe we can an example from Mary in the passage we have read this morning.

1. Going into 2019 we need to reflect/ponder upon what has been and can be

After Christmas it is a good time to reflect upon what we have seen and heard. I have no doubt each one of us here this morning has heard the Christmas message a number of times during our lives but we must respond to the message we have heard and make it fresh in our hearts.

C.S. Lewis said, "we don't need to be told new ideas so much as we need to be reminded of old truths". Friends, we need to make these old truths become fresh upon our hearts again, I am guilty of not doing this myself, I could easily just read over the Christmas message and that is it, however I need ponder upon the message being said and apply to my daily life.

This Christmas we remember again the true meaning of Christmas. God gave himself for us. He was born as one of us so that each of us might be born again into the family of God. That baby born in Bethlehem almost 2000 years ago is the saviour of all of us. Lets not forget the real reason for Christmas this year.

We had a Christmas Service at our home church in Gillingham, our senior minister got the children to dress up to each part of the story as he read it until the end when he announced there was something missing. There was no BABY! Fortunately there was a two month old baby in the congregation and everybody became excited. Of course this had all be arranged however it did remind me that it is so easy not to ponder upon the message of Christmas and then miss the true meaning. Each Advent, we need to ask the question, "where's the baby?". Where is that baby Jesus in our daily lives? Where is he in our Church, our communities, friends and families.

Mary in the passage we have looked at this morning took time to ponder what had be told to her and she treasured that into her heart, friends as we study scripture we must treasure up what the Lord is saying each time we read his Word, when we treasure and ponder upon his Word, we as individuals and as a Church shall see many lives change and come to know Jesus as their Lord and Saviour. I am convinced as Church in the UK we shall see the Kingdom of God grow if we take time to ponder and treasure up his Word.

I do not know where we as individuals and as a Church have been on our journey in life during 2018 but one thing I do not know, however easy or difficult this year has been, God is still in control and he has a future for us. When we ponder upon God's word is soon becomes apparent that God is in control and has an exciting future for us.

This year has had a lot of positives for us as a family but at the start of the year I was very ill in hospital with my Chrohn's disease, I had a quite a lot of time in a hospital Ward to reflect upon scripture and knew whatever outcome for myself and my family, God is with me and has set eternity in my heart.

This year I have felt God challenging me to apply to begin training next year to become a Baptist Minister, I must add I always said no to this but God has really challenged me, I must admit I am slightly anxious about this, time and time asking myself questions such as, am I capable, what about health, family and whether our home church will vote yes in January? These are negative questions I keep asking myself but each time I study and ponder upon God's Word, I find these negative thoughts disappear.

This morning I promise each and every one of you, if we study and ponder upon God's Word, we truly will have a positive future and not a negative one.

2. **As well pondering upon God's Word we must PRAISE GOD no matter what circumstances we find ourselves in**

One of my hobbies is to study the Second World War and learn from it. My family bought me a book this Christmas which tells of a Protestant Evangelical preacher name Paul Schneider who preached against the Nazi regime, was arrested and had a chance to be freed if he signed to agree to not preach against the Nazi doctrine, he declined and was killed by lethal injection. When you read further into this story you discover within the awful conditions he was under, his Spirit was unbreakable. No matter what happened to him, he continued to PRAISE GOD.

The Shepherds possibly would have been anxious when they were on the way to Bethlehem to find Mary and Joseph but when they met with the Baby Jesus, they left and returned home praising God for all of the things which they had heard and seen.

A number of years ago I had a nervous breakdown and this resulted in myself suffering with major anxiety. It has taken me a number of years to overcome this and I find myself PRAISING GOD for what happened at the time as I have been supporting a number of people going through similar things. I can stand here and testify how hard it is to PRAISE GOD when we are in a very low place however each time we PRAISE GOD we are taking slow steps to get away from that negative place and move forward. At one of my lowest points during that time, I heard a song from a Christian radio channel which spoke of the healing power of Jesus and I found myself PRAISING GOD.

We are expecting our third child next year and that brings a certain amount of anxiety and excitement at the same time. I am sure Mary would have had those feelings during the months leading to Jesus birth and when Jesus arrived she found herself PRAISING GOD, even before the birth when Mary met her cousin Elizabeth who was also expecting a baby, she found herself and Elizabeth PRAISING GOD even to the point where the baby in Elizabeth's womb leapt for joy.

Christmas day our house is full of excitement with the children eager to open their presents. With certain presents we find that after a period of time they just get put to one side and never used again. This Christmas time as we unwrap the true meaning of the season, we must never put that present to one side but continue to celebrate that present which is JESUS in our lives, if that is not enough reason to PRAISE, then what is?

Someone once said, "We have become a generation of people who worship our work, work at our play and play at our worship." PRAISE and worship to Jesus are what we were created for. PRAISE GOD for everything which has been and PRAISE him for everything that will be.

I love verse 20 of the passage we have looked at this morning, "The Shepherds returned, glorifying and praising God for all the things they had heard and seen, **which were just as they had been told.**". Wow, WHICH WERE JUST AS THEY HAD BEEN TOLD, what a promise that was and is for all of us this morning who have a relationship with Jesus and PRAISE him. We have been promised the gift of eternal life with Jesus if we follow and accept him into our hearts, no matter where we are as individuals and as a Church this morning, we have the promise of being with Jesus forever.

3. As we PRAISE GOD we must also PROCLAIM GOD

Treasuring Christ is something we do not by keeping Him to ourselves but by making Him know to the whole world.

Verse 17 of the chapter we have looked at this morning, **"When they had seen him, they spread the Word concerning what had been told them about this child".**

Our society needs Jesus now more than ever. I see this each time I do a shift with the Ambulance Service, the amount of broken lives who have no hope unless we share Jesus to them.

Just like the shepherds who went away that first Christmas to tell everyone they met, there are so many who have yet to come and see Jesus. Like the angels who interrupted the shepherds sleep the world today needs the light of Christ to come and wake us up from our sleep and point us to the one who can truly save.

As a Church and individuals we can do so much more to share Jesus in our daily lives.

This year I have published two children's books and to get them known I am constantly having to market the books, in the same way, we have to continue to share Jesus to everybody we come across in our lives. Sometimes I have found marketing my books can get me feeling rather low if for example there is not must response however I must not let this stop me and continue, in the same way when we share Jesus there will be times of doubt and discouragement but we must continue to spread Jesus to people because Jesus brings hope to the hopeless situation.

Is 9:2 The people walking in darkness have seen a great light; on those living in the land of the shadow of death a light has dawned… For to us a child is born, to us a son is given, and the government will be on his shoulders. And he will be called Wonderful Counsellor, Mighty God, Everlasting Father, Prince of Peace.

We have a Gospel to Proclaim and we can offer the ultimate counsellor to our hurting World.

As we draw a close to our Worship this morning, the final song sums up what should be doing each day as we meet with Jesus:

"O Come let us adore him, Christ the Lord".

When we have met with Jesus we can only but adore him in PRAISE.

Amen.

Sermon Five

Luke 12 v 13-21 (Already would have been read), The Parable of the Rich Fool

On 1st April each year "April Fools" days is celebrated, No one knows for certain, when or where this special day began, but it is celebrated in one form or another, often by other names, in many countries around the world. I remember my first experience of "April Fools" day, I was getting ready for my newspaper round and the newsagent manager kept saying how my shoes laces were undone, me in my innocence believed him and kept looking down at my shoes and wondering if I had gone mad. There have been many practical jokes pulled on folks in recognition of this day. In 2005, the media reported that NASA had discovered water on Mars, and had actual pictures on the official NASA website. Those who went to the NASA website to check it out, found a picture of a glass of water sitting on a Mars candy bar.

It is amazing the foolish things people will believe and do. Perhaps none is sadder, or more common, than one we find discussed in the 12th chapter of Luke.

The word which sticks out in my mind from this passage is the word **"Fool"**, the word fool means, a person who acts unwisely or imprudently; in other words a silly person. The word "Fool" is not used lightly in Scripture, **Matthew 5:22 But I say unto you, That whosoever is angry with his brother without a cause shall be in danger of the judgment: and whosoever shall say to his brother, Raca, shall be in danger of the council: but whosoever shall say, Thou fool, shall be in danger of hell fire.**

I believe there are some very important lessons which we can take from this passage:

1. **A "Foolish Person" is blinded by lies** – Recently where I serve as Chaplain (South East Coast Ambulance Service) we have started a new venture called JRU unit, which stands for joint response unit and it is a unit which combines Police and Ambulance on Friday and Saturday nights, I had the honour of going out with the JRU unit a couple of weeks ago and we were called to a particular family who had called the Ambulance service out on a number of occasions with what could have been dealt with quite easily by their Doctor, upon visiting the family one of the relatives implied to us that they had lied to the caller handler each time so that they could by pass the waiting, which of course does not work.

When I was reflecting upon the passage we have read this morning this experience I had working with the JRU unit reminded me of the "Foolishness" of lying and the hurt which can and does get caused by lying. There are many times in scripture we read about the negative results of lying:

Eve was blinded in the Garden. Traded paradise for pain.

David was blinded on top of his palace. If I only have that woman, I'll be happy. Traded God's blessing for misery.

Solomon, If I keep these women happy, then I'll be happy. Wrong. If you do what God has called you to do, then you will have the peace you are seeking.

In the children's talk earlier we saw how the media bombard us with "the more we have the more we can get" kind of mentality and if I have more stuff, it will make me content but we never say it like that. We say, "I really want this …" believing the lies on TV that this new car, this bigger house, these whiter teeth, or shinier hair will make me more happy. **These adverts are a Lie and we must learn to be content with what we have.**

2. **The foolish person forgets others** – The rich fool we have looked at this morning in Luke had the approach of just himself when in fact as Jesus followers we are called to do the opposite:

Galations 6:2 – Bear one another's burdens

Ephesians 44:32 Be kind to one another, forgive one another

Colossians 3:16 – teach & admonish one another

1 Thessalonians 4:18 Comfort one another

Hebrews 10:24 Consider one another

1 Peter 3:8 Have compassion on one another

Galatians 5:13 Serve one another

Romans 12:10 Be kindly affectioned one to another with brotherly love: in honour preferring one another.

Recently I have been studying about the life of Martin Luther King, for those of you who may not have heard of Martin Luther King, he was an American Baptist minister and activist who became the most visible spokesperson and leader in the civil rights movement from 1954 until his death in 1968. King is best known for advancing civil rights through nonviolence and civil disobedience, tactics his Christian beliefs. What strikes me as a Dad myself looking at Martin Luther King's life, is how he could have chosen the easy life and lived a quiet life with his young family yet he chose to fight injustice and as a result lost his life, that is the exact attitude Jesus is calling each one of us, not one of being a FOOL and forgetting others but in fact putting others before ourselves. There were many wonderful quotes which Martin Luther King quoted but the one which stood out in my mind this morning was, **I have decided to stick with love. Hate is too great a burden to bear.** When we say a lie we are actually doing the opposite to love and that becomes a burden upon us, we must put Love first, lying ultimately can and does lead to hate whether that is hate within ourselves or others.

3. **The foolish person forgets the future** – The rich fool had not prepared himself for the real, lasting, eternal future.

How many times in life are we tempted to say the odd white lie here and there to get us out of an immediate sticky situation? - In fact when we do this we actually are making the situation worse long term. For example we may say to our teacher when asked if we have completed our homework, yes, when in fact we know we have not even attempted it, the teacher will eventually find out you have been lying and the situation will become worse for yourself.

We all have a choice in life and I always remember a mentor growing up had a saying which has stuck in my mind, "you win or you lose by the way you choose".

The rich fool had a choice and he chose the wrong way and as a result he lost out.

If we focus upon the future rather than here and now of "I want more" approach we are obeying the commands of Jesus.

This morning each one of us is called to make the correct choice and that choice is to follow Jesus, to show compassion and love to one another, when we do this we are actually preparing more for our eternal future and what an amazing future that will be.

The last song which we shall be singing is called "I will offer up my life", when we offer our life to Jesus we shall see many great things happen both now and in eternity and remember when we make the decision to follow Jesus that he is, the same yesterday, today and forever, what a hope we all have this morning.

Amen.

Sermon Six

Genesis 15 v 1-17

C.H Spurgeon in his sermon on 11th June 1874 said the following, "Perhaps the fearful one is some young person who has a relative who hates religion, and what this powerful relative may do they cannot imagine; or the oppressor is an arbitrary employer, and if his employees don't obey his orders exactly, even though those orders happen to be wrong, they will lose their jobs. They may be out of work for months, and they and their children may then go without food. They imagine a long series of trials and troubles that will come upon them because of the wrath of the oppressor. But, in the end, isn't there a great deal more attention given to this matter than there should be, for "where is the wrath of the oppressor?"

There have been many occasions in my life where I can relate to what C H Spurgeon was saying in his sermon all those years ago, for example I can imagine negative outcomes within my own mind but in fact the end result is very positive. During these times of anxiety/fear I have personally not trusted in God as much as I should have and it is only later that I can really see where God was in it all.

In my own personal study time with the Lord I am working through the book of Genesis and very much felt led to speak on the chapter which we have looked at this morning. In particular I was drawn to verse 1 where God said to Abram, "Do not be afraid, Abram, I am your shield, your very great reward.

I believe we can take a number of lessons from the passage we have read this morning.

1. It is very tempting to give into fear but we must recognise that God is with us no matter what our circumstances are.

Before God had said these Words, "Do not be afraid" to Abram, Abram had just returned to the Valley of Shaveh after defeating the King of Elam and the kings allied with him. Abram would have been in a fearful state of mind after a major battle and immediately is greeted by the King of Sodom who offers him a substantial award. Recognising that God was with him within the battle, Abram's response was to not take the whole reward offered but to share it out equally.

There are times in life when we just give into that temptation of fear. I want to personally share part of own testimony this morning about how I gave into fear and how God was with me all along.

In 2008 a child from my Dad's church in Dartford was tragically killed by a bus, I helped support the young people at the Church including the boys brother. It was not until a year later I would get images/flashbacks in my mind of how that boy was killed, on top of this I had moved into our first marital home and I felt a lot of pressure. I started to suffer major anxiety and ended up not leaving our house due to fear of the unknown. Eventually after therapy and counselling I was able to rebuild my life and get back to work and later go on to start Chaplaincy work supporting other people going through similar experiences. At the time it I as riddled with fear, fear of the unknown but I was able to get through this with support from my wife, family, friends and Church. I look back at that time now and I thank God for that time as I have learned to face any fear which life brings by trusting God and his Word.

This morning, I do not know where as individuals and as a church where we are at but each one of us faces various different kinds of fear during our lifetime. The promise God made to Abram about being his shield and reward, he has that same promise this morning for each and everyone of us who accept Jesus as our Lord and Saviour. No matter what circumstances we find ourselves in, we have that reassurance that God is with us.

There is a meaning to the word fear and that is, **Face Every Anxiety Right on**, I would add to this meaning this morning, **Face Every Anxiety Right on With God On Your Side.**

The reward which God spoke to Abram was a reward that God was with him not only during his life on this earth but also in heaven for eternity. We also have that reward when we accept God into our lives and I cannot think of anything more rewarding than eternity with my Lord and Saviour. There are many earthly pleasures which we can enjoy, for example when my children receive a present for Christmas or a birthday, they cannot leave those presents alone but not long after the presents end up on a shelf never to be used again. Our reward for following Jesus goes far beyond a temporary satisfaction and lasts forever.

We have that promise from God, that no matter what our circumstances are, we do not need to be afraid because God is with us.

2. When we trust God, the future for us as a Church and Individuals will be exciting

Abram still has some doubts about these promises that God makes to him. After all it had been about 10 years since God had promised that his descendants would become a great nation and Abram still didn't have a son.

When we look further into the life of Abram we see that Abram became known as Abraham and his wife became known as Sarah, this was because Abraham was given a covenant by God that he would be the father of many nations. At 100 years old Abraham became a Father to a son called Isaac.

Yes, along our journey in this life, we will have our doubts and fears at times, no doubt Abram had doubts and fears yet the purposes of God were worked through in his life and many lives have been touched since.

It excites me this morning to think that God can use us here to draw others to him. I think of the words of Jesus when he said, " I will never leave you nor forsake you". We could be feeling for example this morning that numbers at our church are low, this is irrelevant really because when we trust God, like the life of Abraham, we will see many descendants who come to know Jesus as their Lord and Saviour.

Recently a colleague within the Ambulance service has started to attend our home church regularly, he was certain that there was no such thing as God this time last year, since attending our church, he missed one Sunday service and said, "I was gutted to not be at the service". When we trust God and follow him, others will be drawn to us and ultimately that draws people to God. James 4v8, "Draw near to God and he will draw near to you". When we put fear and doubt aside and draw near to God, we will see the Kingdom of God grow, that excites me.

3. Faith in God's promises conquers

V6 of Genesis 15, Abram believed the Lord, and he credited it to him as righteousness.

Abram believed God and that because of his faith God credits that belief to him as righteousness. It is this verse that reveals to us the key principle from this passage, Faith in God's promises conquers.

Paul in the New Testament in the book of Romans (8v37) also makes it clear that Faith in God's promises conquers, **No, in all these things we are more than conquerors through him who loved us.**

I spoke a little earlier about my own journey which I would describe as a breakdown in my life. During that period I was in our house and I heard a lovely song which spoke of the healing power of Jesus and how he overcame, it was at that point I knelt beside my bed and said, "Lord, I cannot cope any more, I trust you, if you have a purpose still for me in this life please lift this burden of anxiety from me. The journey afterwards has been hard at times but I can say this morning that I have conquered many fears, I stopped preaching for a number of years due to fear and this morning gives testimony to how through Jesus we are more than conquerors.

Abram would have had doubts about becoming the Father of many nations yet later on he became a father and so the promise was God was and is fulfilled.

When we cast aside all fears and doubts, we begin to see God's purposes being worked out, even through those difficult times God's purposes are being worked through.

One of my favourite Psalms which really has helped me conquer my fears is **Psalm 46 v 1-3, God is our refuge and strength, an ever-present help in trouble. Therefore we will not fear, though the earth give way and the mountains fall into the heart of the sea, though it's waters roar and foam and the mountains quake with their surging.**

It is interesting to see throughout the whole Bible that God is with us along our journey in this life and that we can conquer anything which this life throws at us.

I love Chapter 6 in the book of Ephesians where we are called to take up the armour of God, **Finally, be strong in the Lord and in his mighty power. Put on the full armour of God, so that you can take your stand against the devil's schemes. For our struggle is not against flesh and blood, but against the rulers, against the authorities, against the powers of this dark world and against the spiritual forces of evil in the heavenly realms. Therefore put on the full armour of God, so that when the day of evil comes, you may be able to stand** your ground, and after you have done everything, to stand. Stand firm then, with the belt of truth buckled around your waist, with the breastplate of righteousness in place, and with your feet fitted with the readiness that comes from the gospel of peace. In addition to all this, take up the shield of faith, with which you can extinguish all the flaming arrows of the evil one. Take the helmet of salvation and the sword of the Spirit, which is the word of God.

The shield of protection which Abram was promised is also the protection offered by God to us in the book of Ephesians.

When we put on this armour of God, the words God spoke to Abram will also be for us, "Do not be Afraid".

As we enter each new day, it is a healthy thing to pray that we are shielded with the armour of God, shielded so that all of our fears and doubts are gone, when we see this happen, we will truly become more than conquerors.

I have chosen our closing song to be, "When heavenly armour enters the land, the battle belongs to the Lord".

All of the fears and doubts which we have, let us take that armour and let God take control of our battles, when we do this, we will see amazing things happen in our lives and as a church.

Amen.

Sermon Seven

Matthew 28 v 16-20

God is still building his church through People.

And I tell you that you are Peter, and on this rock I will build my church, and the gates of Hades will not overcome it. - Matthew 16:18

What a shocking statement our Lord makes. Here Jesus tells a fisherman that he is the rock that he will build his Church. You would think Jesus would have picked a theologian, Pharisee or some other religious expert but he chosen a simple, rough, zealous fisherman. Perhaps it was Peter's child-like faith, or his determination to stand for the Lord at all times. Perhaps the Lord was thinking this fellow gets it wrong all the time so if the Church is established in his leadership everyone will know its a miracle and God working not a man. Either way or for whatever reason the Lord makes this statement that he would give him the "keys of the kingdom of heaven" (Matthew 16:19). It does seem clear in the wording he is speaking first person to Peter the entire time, then he started to speak to all the disciples, "Then he ordered his disciples not to tell anyone that he was the Messiah" (Matthew 16:20). What is important to realise here is that God's plan is to use imperfect people to accomplish his purposes on the earth. The plan of God is the Church and there is no alternative or other method for spreading his Good News.

This morning we are looking at the subject of "A time for building" and I believe God is saying to us this morning that he will build his church through his people.

I believe there are a number of things we can take from this mornings passage:

1. Building the Kingdom of God takes time and often God allows us to wait so that we grow in him

We live in a society which wants things done NOW. The Ambulance Service is a classic example of this where people expect you to be instantly at their call even though you could be tied up with other incidents. There have been many instances of this which I could talk about this morning but all I can say is that people expect to be fixed FAST and not to be fixed fast often gets taken out on myself and my colleagues.

If we are to build the Kingdom of God here in Meopham and further a field we must learn this one particular fruit of the Spirit, Patience, Galations 5 v 22.

Show picture of GBC Building Project

Explain – This is our home church and currently we are under going a major building project which will make a statement to a needy community that we are here for you, the project has taken many years to get to this stage and has had plenty of frustrations along the way. There have been times when we have doubted for example the cost of the project yet God has now allowed the project to go ahead and the finances have and are coming together. This has taken a lot of time and patience.

As an individual and as a church I know at times we have got pretty frustrated and wondered what the future holds for the physical building and I believe this had to happen in order for us to develop the fruit of the Spirit of Patience within us as a Body of Christ in Gillingham.

Verse 17 of Matthew 28 shows us that the Disciples even doubted and Jesus response is that which has impacted many lives and continues to do so. Waiting does put doubt into our minds but in time we will reap the benefits of waiting and see the Kingdom of God grow not just physically as a building but within the many lives which we will see and we will see these many lives come to know Jesus as their personal Lord and Saviour.

2. **If we are to Build the Kingdom of God we must work together with other brothers and sisters not just within one church**

After the EU vote the Methodist Church released a very lovely statement which said, "We must work together for a better today and a better tomorrow, many people shared different views recently on the vote, some were upset, some were angry and many arguments occurred, as a body of Christ we are called to be United and whatever we voted and our views are we are called to be United as one church in a World which is very not united. It was clear from the voting that the United Kingdom was not as United as we first thought".

If we are to be serious about the Great Commission to Baptist people of all Nations, personalities etc we must Unite with our Brothers and Sisters in Christ and put our differences a side. In a wounded World people are looking for security, Love and if we are not United people will not be drawn to us.

As I was typing my sermon I was responding at the same time to something on Social media which has caused a lot of upset between a few people, I just add it had nothing to do with myself but my own opinions were sought. My response was that whatever our differences we must work together for the better. Like or hate Social Media it is here and to stay, there are many negatives to Social Media with people arguing and having differences, families and friends have been destroyed as a result of some things said on Social Media. Likewise, I have seen and heard of many churches destroyed due to not being so united in Christ and we must work together for the Kingdom of God not against one another.

Jesus Spoke to not just one person about the Great Commission but a group of people and then encouraged them to Spread the Word of God to many people. The disciples would have been united as a group and worked together to make Disciples of all Nations baptising them in the Name of the Father, Son and Holy Spirit.

As many of you know I have published a book and have another one which is due out in the next 4 weeks, I have formed a limited company as I cannot make this venture succeed on my own but stands a better chance with more people working alongside me, in the same way we are called to work together as a team within our local and national churches and I know that when we do this the Kingdom of God will increase.

Good things do and can come from conflict if we put aside our differences, as I mentioned a short while ago I had an issue with Social Media while preparing this mornings message and what is interesting to see is that people are asking me many questions about my faith as a result.

3. If we are to work together for the Kingdom we must have the FAITH in Jesus

Faith is the evidence of things not seen.

James 1 v 2-4, "Consider it pure joy, my brothers, whenever you face trials of many kinds, because you know that the testing of your faith develops Perseverance Perseverance must finish it's work so that you may be mature and complete, lacking nothing".

You can't build up your faith if you're constantly given things as soon as you ask for them. This is important because faith is something that brings great honour and glory to God. Moments of faith are moments when we believe in God for who He is rather than what He's done. I cannot build up faith if I'm never required to exercise faith. I have said previously about the transfusions which I am receiving for Chrohns disease and the anxiety I had around that initially but I had to make the decision to step out in Faith and Believe this was part of the journey towards healing within myself. I know whatever the outcome long term that God is with me and not against me.

Faith is not always an instant thing as we would like it, it may take years to work together with somebody but having the Faith to take that step towards working together and seeking healing and forgiveness will reap it's benefits. Once the first hurdle has been accomplished we will begin to reap the benefits of working together.

I recently heard a song which said, " when the final curtains close, you reap what you sow". Friends, when our final curtain closes upon our earthly life do we want to be remembered for not working together for the Kingdom of God or be remembered as a Disciple of God seeking to build the Kingdom of God? By seeking to build the Kingdom of God we must take that step of Faith and put aside our differences and work together for a better tomorrow.

We tend to view waiting like a battery. I have certain amount of power and the longer God makes me wait the more depleted I am. This is so untrue and we must take the step of Faith that in God's time and not ours that he will work things for the good and for the extension of his Kingdom both here in Meopham and further a field.

Consider an alternative image: a pregnancy. Pregnancy also requires waiting, but the longer you're waiting, the more the child is growing and maturing. In essence, with a pregnancy, the waiting doesn't diminish; it increases and what an outcome this brings. I look at our two sons this morning and remember the long 9 months wait, anticipation of being a first time parent, then other anticipations for the second child, those 9 months were quite frightening and exciting at the same time. Likewise, if we take that Step of Faith this morning we will get times of doubt, worry and excitement but we must trust that by exercising Faith within our lives and as a church, that the Kingdom of God will grow.

There is the thought that's in the back of our minds. Maybe He's not paying attention any more. Maybe He's busy somewhere else. But remember we have a promise that Jesus will never leave us or forsake us, Hebrews 13v5, **"Never will I leave you, never will I forsake you"**. This is important to hold onto in the midst of our waiting so that we know He has legitimate reasons for the delay.

Will you trust Him today?

Sermon Eight

Exodus 12:12-17

A time for celebrating.

The story of the Exodus from the clutches of Pharaoh is well-known. Moses had been commissioned to lead the Israelites from Egypt but Pharaoh was loathe to leave them go as they were a valuable source of free labour in his building projects. They were held in slavery, and were forced to submit to hard labour, to suffer unrestrained beatings and to make bricks without straw. Demonstrations of God's power in inflicting successive plagues of increasing intensity and discomfort to Egypt's infrastructure only served to harden Pharaohs heart. God had to move against him, in the words of the historian, with 'an outstretched arm and with mighty acts of judgement' (Exodus 6:6).

The Israelites were instructed to mark the doorposts of their homes with the blood of a slaughtered spring lamb and, upon seeing this, the spirit of the Lord knew to *pass over* the first-born in these homes, hence the English name of the holiday.

When the Pharaoh freed the Israelites, it is said that they left in such a hurry that they could not wait for bread dough to rise (leaven). In commemoration, for the duration of Passover no leavened bread is eaten, for which reason Passover is called the **feast of unleavened bread** in the Torah or Old Testament.

Some dates or events stick in the mind because of the historical association it has, to us or our community: 14th July 2007 sticks in my mind as this was the day myself and Caroline got married, I dare not forget this date each year. Historical Occasions are special because of their uniqueness and importance, whether good or otherwise. Festivals are celebrated in religion to remind their followers that something special happened. The institution of the Passover was, and still is, very important to the Jews as it reminded them of a Red Letter Day in the history of emerging nation of Israel. It was the starting point of their exodus from slavery in Egypt and a milestone in their learning journey in their knowledge of God. In fact the Passover is a self-disclosure of God at a crucial moment in their history.

For the Christian, the Passover isn't a festival as such, but for what it represents as a symbol of redemption. Here we see a foreshadowing of Jesus as the Lamb of God, the Saviour of the world to as many as would believe in Him.

I believe there are a number of lessons we can take from this passage today:

1. **We can be set free from the burdens we face in our daily lives both as individuals and as a church**

Our youngest son Daniel has a real fear of one of my colleagues and recently my colleague picked Daniel up in his arms and he would not stop screaming until I picked him up. In the Same, if we offer our lives this morning to God the burdens we have will be taken away from us and we will get that peace which we need.

Life can at times offer some real challenging situations for us and we have two choices, we can either run away from our problems or face them. One of the things I learned through counselling to myself and now to others I am helping, is to face a fear head on is the best way long term, to start with it is very hard to face a fear but the more we face our fears the easier it becomes. When we do this the fear eventually becomes lifted from us and in the same way if we are to come before the Lamb of God and trust him our burden's will be set free.

When burdens are lifted from us it becomes the dawning of a new day and the beginning of a new life.

Whenever you read or hear the words "redeem" or "redemption" in the New Testament, they speak of freedom from slavery.

Whenever you mention words like Deliverance,Bondage,or Redemption to the Jews they immediately think of Passover and Israel's deliverance from Egypt through the blood of the lamb.

Whenever you mention words like Deliverance,Bondage,or Redemption to the Christian right away we begin to think of the Sacrifice that Jesus made on the cross to set us free from the enemy. He was a Passover Lamb as well.

Many years after the passover we find Jesus and the 12 Disciples partaking of the Passover Feast. We also know this as the Last Supper. There at the Last Supper Jesus explained to them that this was to be the Last Passover and that a "New day" was coming. That new day is for us new life with a future of our burdens being lifted from us.

Jesus wants to set us from from our burdens this morning both as individuals and as a church.

2. **The Lord's table is to be taken seriously in order for our burdens to be lifted**

We have looked at the passover meal and the significance that has both for us as individuals and as a church.

There are two principles we see in the Passover Meal:

1. Through the blood of the lamb Israel was released from slavery, the kingdom of darkness, judgement.

2. The eating of the lamb had to do with physical strength and nourishment.

The blood deals with issues of sin and rebellion.

Eating lamb deals with physical issues, healing and health.

Two fold purpose of Jesus death on the cross:

1. Forgiveness of our sins through the blood of Christ

Eph 1:7 In Him we have redemption through His blood, the forgiveness of our trespasses, according to the riches of His grace.

2. Healing/Health through his physical suffering

Mtt 8:16-17 . When evening came, they brought to Him many who were demon-possessed; and He cast out the spirits with a word, and healed all who were ill.

When we take communion this is a celebration meal which is to be taken seriously and not lightly.

To benefit from Communion- must be seen as more than a ritual- it is a life-giving experience.

Communion- fellowship, partnership, participation.

Can also be seen as communication; He speaks, we listen, we speak, He listens.

The whole purpose of the Passover meal was to convince Pharaoh to let Israel go free and this morning, when we consider each time we partake in communion we know we can be set free, set free from our burdens/sin and have new life in Jesus.

You would have heard me say a prayer at the end of each communion service I have led – Worthy is the lamb who was slain, to receive power and wealth and wisdom and might and honour and glory and blessing. To him who sits upon the throne and to the lamb, be blessing and honour and glory and might for ever and ever. Amen.

When we take this approach coming to the Lord's table we shall leave this building with new life.

3. After the Communion feast we must celebrate

Psalm 103: 1-3. Bless the LORD, O my soul, And all that is within me, bless His holy name. Bless the LORD, O my soul, And forget none of His benefits; Who pardons all your iniquities, Who heals all your diseases.

These are the benefits that we have as a result of the sacrifice that Jesus made on the cross for us.

Insurance Policies - How you have to read small print with excess etc, Jesus has become our eternal insurance policy and with Jesus there is no small print.

However we come to communion, whether low or high, there is a sense of real joy afterwards and a sense of new life.

I love it when we have communion at our home church as EVERYBODY of all ages is welcome to participate in communion, it is very important to me that this happens as we are one big family and if the youngest to oldest know what they are doing they should be welcome to participate.

Revelation 3:20 – Behold, I stand at the door and knock; if anyone hears my voice and opens the door, I will come in to him and eat with him, and he with me.

The invitation to participate in communion extends to everybody who loves the Lord Jesus and is in need of Heavens Love and forgiveness.

I often follow a book called "Orders and prayers for church Worship" and there is a prayer in this book which I really love and is for the ending of communion, "Go forth in the World in peace; be of good courage; hold fast that which is good; render to no man evil for evil; strengthen the faint hearted; support the weak; help the afflicted; honour all men; love and serve the Lord, rejoicing in the power of the Holy Spirit Amen.

Amen

Sermon Nine

Acts 3

The Book of Acts focuses upon the beginnings of the church, and two particular people. The apostle Peter and Paul the Apostle. The Gospel spreaded from Israel, northward to Antioch, and then westward to Asia Minor, Greece, and finally Rome, the heart of the Roman Empire. The first 12 chapters of the book of Acts deal with Peter, and the remainder of the book, the last 16 chapters is devoted to the apostle Paul. One of the key areas which the author (which is Luke) has dealt with within the first seven chapters is the establishment and progress of the church in Jerusalem until the dispersion which arose around the time of Stephen's death.

As I was preparing this morning's message I very much felt it laid upon my heart to encourage us as a church for the future and coming back together both physically and virtually. This pandemic has created a lot of fear in all of us and I can totally understand the feeling of apprehension and fear as we look to come back together within our church building.

I believe as we look ahead there are a number of things we can take from the passage which we have looked at this morning.

1. **First and foremost it is through prayer that we are guided by making the right decisions and feeling the peace which takes away that fear**

A mother was teaching her 3-year-old the Lord's prayer. For several evenings at bedtime she repeated it after her mother. One night she said she was ready to solo. The mother listened with pride as she carefully enunciated each word, right up to the end of the prayer. "Lead us not into temptation," she prayed, "but deliver us some e-mail, Amen."

I love humour and we can come to God in prayer innocent like a child and we can guarantee he will listen even if we don't quite get the answer we were hoping for.

Peter and John would have been very disciplined in their prayer life as Jews because the Jews had three daily times of prayer. In this the passage we have looked at this morning Peter and John went to the temple to pray at three in the afternoon which was the 'hour of prayer' being the ninth hour and the other two were 9:00 a.m. (third hour) and 12:00 noon (sixth hour). Wow!

I must confess this morning my own prayer life at times is not as what it should be. Life can get busy and I can find myself neglecting my communication with God each day. There are so many different ways we pray to God no matter how busy our lives can get. For example we can pray quietly during the day, out loud or with others but it is essential that we spend time in prayer daily as individuals and regularly as a church family.

Recently I visited a somebody and part of that visit we needed to pop out to a shop to purchase a computer part, as we entered into the shop the lady froze, shaking and had a panic attack. She shared with me that this was due to not going out for over a year with the pandemic and it all seemed daunting for her. After talking the lady through deep breathing exercises and reassuring her, she was able to carry on with purchasing the part and felt quite confident afterwards. I am aware for some of us listening this morning that there could concerns about when and how we meet back up as a church physically. I would urge you to pray over this fear first of all and then share those concerns with the leaders so more prayer can go into it. It is through prayer that answers are revealed and peace is found. As I have shared before, we may not get the answers in ways we would like or looking for but we can be assuring that God is listening and knows exactly what he is doing.

1 Peter 5:7, NIV: "Cast all your anxiety on him because he cares for you." Peter writes that we should take that fear and cast it—throw it—onto our Father God. In fact, he tells us to take all of our anxieties, everything that worries us, and to give it to the God who cares so deeply for us.

This is not a promise that God will fix everything which worries us. God is not obligated to follow whatever script we write for Him. It's a promise that the mighty God will receive our worries, and care about them. He will carry them for us. He is trustworthy to handle them in the way that is best.

Peter's words are a command. It is not God's will for His children to continue to live under those burdens.

Believing that God is mighty and cares for us should result in our regularly handing over our worries to Him.

When the time comes for meeting back physically in the church if you find yourself worried as you enter into the building, take a deep breath in and out , praying to God for peace at the same time and so the same applies to wherever we find ourselves in life. I am saying this as somebody who has suffered major anxiety in the past and from time to time continue to suffer with. I am slowing learning myself to be more disciplined with my prayer life handing this to God.

2. I believe as we gradually meet back together that healing is going to take place

The man at the temple who was crippled from birth and begged daily was very much looking for healing in the wrong way. Looking at Peter and John he was expecting them to provide silver and gold but I love Peter's response when he says, **'silver or gold I do not have but what I give you in the name of Jesus Christ of Nazareth, walk'.**

In the West we have got very materialised and if this pandemic has taught us one thing as a society and that is, 'what are our priorities?'.

I believe we even as a church (in general) we have lost our ways at times and gone about things in the wrong ways, we can get so bogged down with what really are minor things and neglect the essential things such as prayer and loving one another. Friends, it is important as we come together that we look to Jesus and seek his face. **Matthew 6:33: But seek ye first the kingdom of God, and his righteousness; and all these things shall be added unto you.**

It must have been an amazing thing for the beggar to have been healed after spending so much time asking for silver and gold yet the answer was right in front of him being the temple which ultimately points to God. It is essential that we gather back together at some point as a church as there are many hurting people that walk past our church daily and by being here for them we are helping them to see Jesus and that ultimately brings the healing which is so badly needed. These people who walk past may not be crippled physically like the beggar was but they are crippled with all of the things which this World has and we need to be the church of God which welcomes them and gives them that hope and healing which only can be found in Jesus.

I remember a conversation with a member of the church I briefly was pasturing one morning in the week when the coffee shop was open and this particularly member was saying how discouraging it is that we are open twice a week and yet not many people enter in. That same day a lady came in who was not known to any of us and she was really hurting, we were able to pray and listen, seeing a difference in her after she left. We may feel discouraged but it is not about numbers it is about people as individuals. It is my firm belief that if we lead one person to Jesus then that is a fantastic thing and Kingdom building. With the restrictions as they are of course we are limited but remember if one life is healed and comes to know Jesus that is doing what we are called to do as a church.

Don't forget when healing takes place it is essential to thank and praise God for this just like the beggar did.

3. We should not be surprised what God has in store for us both as individuals and as a church

When the beggar was walking and praising God in the temple the people were amazed at what they were seeing before their eyes. Peter immediately challenges the people and questioned why they should be surprised. Peter would have been very bold doing this and in particular challenging the people in the temple how they handed Jesus over to Pilate to be crucified.

Each time I re read the account of Jesus death and resurrection is always stands out to me how one day the people welcomed Jesus shouting, 'hosanna blessed is he who is comes in the name of the Lord' and then a few days later shout, 'crucify'. And so that kind of attitude has continued throughout history where one minute we can be all for somebody or something and then the next condemn. BUT we can change that thinking today by the forgiveness each one of us has through Jesus death on the cross. We must ask forgiveness upon ourselves if we have wronged anybody and secondly asked forgiveness for those who has wronged us. Luke 6:37 **Judge not, and ye shall not be judged: condemn not, and ye shall not be condemned: forgive, and ye shall be forgiven.**

When we seek this forgiveness we should not be surprised by what God has in store for us as individuals and as a church.

I say this as somebody has been hurt by people in the past both at church and bullying growing up. For too long my own heart has held grudges at times and I have had to come to a place of asking God for forgiveness both upon myself and the ones who have wronged me. I have personally found that this has bought a lot of healing and new doors opening up which I never anticipated. So it is with each and every one of us this morning as we look to the future we should not be surprised what God has in store for us and the hope which that brings to this broken World.

I am sure each and every one of us this morning can share of times in our lives where we can been astonished at the things which God has done for us and for others. God is still on the throne and he has not lost control.

Peter in his challenge to the people at the temple urged them to repent and turn to Christ. Each and every one of us this morning has that very special gift offered to us which nothing in this World can offer and as we look to come back together as a fellowship, we can share that special gift of knowing Jesus to our community.

Sermon Ten

Reading: Luke 13: 10-17

"A crippled woman healed on the Sabbath"

Introduction – I serve as Chaplain to South East Coast Ambulance Service and my role is quite varied from attending long shifts with the crew and being at the station to be a listening ear, in particular I spend a lot of time supporting colleagues who are suffering with PTSD and being there for them as and when required. I have even recently published a children's book called "Paramedic Chris" which is based upon the work which the crew do.

More recently I have been attending more shifts with the crew and not that long ago I was on duty on a Sunday which was a new experience for myself as I have never attended a shift on a Sunday before. I was able to see first hand what time people in Medway wake up! Jokes aside the following Sunday at a Church service I would find myself coming into criticism from an individual for working the previous Sunday, when I was preparing this mornings message the passage we have looked at reminded me of the comment which I received after doing a Sunday shift. In the passage which we have read, on a Sabbath day Jesus heals a woman who has been crippled for 18 years and the synagogue ruler is indignant and tells the assembled people not to come on a Sabbath Day to be healed. Jesus response is wonderful as he calls them hypocrites – they are willing on the Sabbath to untie their Donkey so it might have water, yet not for the needy who need to be healed.

I believe there are number of lessons which we can take from this today:

1. **We must demonstrate compassion to ourselves as individuals as well as to others** – The woman was crippled was 18 years, she would have had issues with being bent over and general mobility additionally to this other people would have looked down on her. At that time many people would have believed her condition was a result of sin, Jesus instead connects with her suffering and instead of condemning her immediately heals her. I wonder how much compassion during those 18 years the lady had upon herself, did she suffer with things such as depression, low self esteem, anger? I suspect she did as a physical condition like this would really test any of us let alone all of the condemning which took place. Too many times within my Chaplaincy work I have seen people put down by others and this has led the individual to go into themselves and as a result they have closed the door to compassion to themselves as well as from others.

A number of years ago I was diagnosed with Chrohns disease and as a result I went into myself and blamed myself, was it the food I ate, stress I could not handle, the questions kept coming and coming into my mind. I was showed a lot of compassion at the time by church friends and family but had no compassion upon myself – the compassion which says that God loves me and we must learn to love ourselves more as a result of this.

Recently I undertook some mental health training with Secamb and I learned a worrying statistic that one in three people suffer from depression, friends there many people within our society today who we can reach out to by showing compassion and that God loves them, it can be simple things such as taking somebody out for a coffee, shopping, listening to them or weekly visits but all of these actions demonstrate compassion and God's love.

As well as ourselves we are called to show compassion and love to everybody, **2 Corinthians 1:4, "He brings us alongside someone else who is going through hard times so that we can be there for that person".** When we come alongside somebody like this it is amazing to witness the healing which takes place and this may not be an immediate healing, in fact in my experience it takes time for the healing process to take place.

1 Corinthians 13:13, **"And Now these three remain, faith, hope and love. But the greatest of these is love"**. In the NIV Bible the word LOVE appears 559 times in the Old and New Testament. Just as Jesus demonstrated his love in the story which we have read about this morning we must show that same love to everybody we meet within our daily lives. If I was at the Synagogue when the woman was healed I would have had a massive celebration but the rulers instead questioned Jesus and as a result the people in the crowd were offended but Jesus took the opportunity to reach out to the crowd and show them what really matters to God.

I recently celebrated my birthday and one of the presents I received was a classical car magazine, one of the articles was on a very old car which had been sitting in ruins for a number of years, a team of mechanics upon seeing the car decided to get together and restore the car to it's original condition, what started out as a rust bucket now looks amazing. In the same way when we do not show love to ourselves we are like the rusted car but when we come to a place where we love ourselves we have rebuilt ourselves to what God has called us to be.

2. There was a Spiritual Battle going on when the rulers questioned Jesus – Verse 15-17 of the passage we have read this morning Jesus answers the rulers when they question him and I personally believe Jesus was being guided at this stage in how he responded as clearly there was a Spiritual battle going on. There are three things I believe we can learn this morning when we are going through Spiritual battles:

Use our Spiritual resources - "God is our refuge and Strength" - Psalm 46v1. God's word illuminates the darkness and confusion which we often find ourselves in, when I have been unwell myself particularly with Chrohn's disease it is easy for myself to go downwards on a mental roller-coaster but I find picking up my Bible counteracts that and the Word of God brings comfort to my body and soul, **Phillipians 4:7, "He gives peace which surpasses all understanding"**. When I study God's word more and more I find I connect Spiritually to God and this brings things such as depressive feelings into perspective.

Use our Personal Resources – We must keep remind ourselves and others of our strengths and skills, help to remember past triumph's and keep encouraging that positive attitude. When I am listening to colleagues who are speaking very negative about themselves, I mention about the two sides of the brain, the left and right side, the one side is negative and the other is positive, when a negative thought comes to mind you need to trick that thought so that it goes to the positive side of the brain. Using our Personal resources will help us overcome our Spiritual battles and again I would urge to increase Bible study time and prayer time.

Use our interpersonal Resources – By this I mean people such as family members, friends, neighbours and our Church community/family. Last week our oldest son had an accident, gently I was able to come alongside him and reassure him everything was OK and we will sort it out together, he has got to the age now where he feels embarrassment over these kind of things and is reluctant to ask for help. I also have at times felt embarrassed in various situations to seek help due to worry of what others think for example but actually my experience tells me that there is nothing to be embarrassed about as people are generally more understanding than what we realise. In our Spiritual battles we must use these interpersonal resources.

3. **We must position ourselves to receive** – Proverbs 12v15, "**The wise listen to others**". There was a saying I learned growing up which went, "we win or we lose by the way we choose", although the the crippled lady was approached by Jesus, I believe that she had it within her heart that she wanted to be healed and she had the choice to say "Yes" to Jesus. I wonder if any of the rulers and the crowd who criticised Jesus, if they were to become crippled would they have said Yes to Jesus? So many times I find myself questioning where Jesus is in times of crisis yet he is still with us, I make the choice whether to allow Jesus to work within me or not and a big lesson we can take from the crippled woman is the fact that she made the right choice to listen/receive from Jesus. God can and does speaks to us through other people but we must first of all be willing to listen and receive from God.

I was told of a true story which happened in the 1920s, a train broke down in a tunnel and they lost radio contact at both ends of the train, instead of meeting each other physically halfway they started to pull the train at both ends into two different directions which ultimately caused a massive explosion, if they had communicated properly and received each others messages such a disaster would have been avoided, in the same way if we are not willing to listen and to receive from God we will not move forward, we are called to receive from God who is Love, compassionate, faithful.

This morning if we are finding ourselves in that place of suffering, be it physical or mental suffering, we must open our hearts to God to receive his Love, Grace and compassion, if one of my children fall over and hurt themselves they will come and embrace me in my arms and we have a God who's arms are always open to go to for comfort.

The closing song speaks about how we can face tomorrow and future because all fear is gone, when we receive and listen to God we have that reassurance that we can face tomorrow knowing he God is with us.

Amen.

Printed in Great Britain
by Amazon